SPORTS ENCYCLOPEDIA

EQUINE AND MIND SPORTS

Om KIDZ
An imprint of Om Books International

Contents

EQUINE SPORTS

Which child hasn't heard stories of white knights galloping in on a horse to save the day?

The domestication of horses started before 3000 BCE. Since then, horses became an important part of people's lives. They were used for transport and for carrying loads.

Slowly, this practice of breeding horses to achieve better results turned into a competition amongst the breeders. Horses were pitted against each other to compare their desirable traits. Slowly, different breeds became renowned for their different qualities.

Several sports displaying people's skills with horses were also developed. Certain countries can trace back the origin of equine sports to ancient war training.

Some equine sports also came into being as a result of certain herding practices, like those seen in rodeos.

Let's gear up and take a look at some equine sports!

Did you know? The oldest woman to compete in the Olympics was a British dressage rider named Lorna Johnstone. She participated in the 1972 games, at the age of 70.

Polo

All players must wear riding boots which come up just below the knee. They wear white denim trousers.

Polo is a unique team sport played on horseback. In this, the players use a long stick called "mallet" and try to move the ball into the opponent's goal post.

Origin

Polo, which is a game of Central Asian origin, was first played in Persia (modern-day Iran). Its invention dates back to the sixth century BCE, but some sources also believe that it was invented in the first century. This sport was played by both men and women in the court of King Khosrow II Parviz.

From Persia, the game spread to Arabia, from where it spread to Tibet, China and Japan. In the thirteenth century, Muslim conquerers brought the game of Polo to India.

The Calcutta Polo Club was formed in the early 1860s. The game became popular through informal matches. The first international competition took place in 1886, when the USA unsuccessfully challenged the English. Polo used to be a part of the Olympics, but has recently been dropped.

Players tug on the reins of the horses and use a whip to control its movement.

The polo shirts worn by the players have become very popular among the masses.

The polo mallet has a rubber-coated grip which is known as a sling.

The polo saddle is a close-contact jumping saddle without a flap under the billets. Players may choose to use a saddle blanket.

The head of the mallet is made of a hardwood called "tipa". It is cigar-shaped.

Rules

The rules of this sport are strictly enforced to ensure that the players and their horses are safe for the entire duration of the match. The player who hits the ball with a mallet gets the right of way. The other players cannot cross a player who has the right of way. To take possession of the ball, they must approach this player from either side. They can only cross a player if their safety is not under threat.

If a player has possession of the ball, another player can block the swing of their mallet in order to gain possession. This is called "hooking".

This picture shows the mallets and the polo balls that are used during a polo match.

The game begins with the two teams in a line facing each other at the centre of the field. Each team has four members. One of the umpires throws the ball between the participating teams. The team which gets the ball, passes it between its team mates. With speed and strategy, each team tries to score or block the opponents.

A player may use two or three different ponies in low goal matches. Four or more are common for medium goal matches. The highest levels of competition may have more than one pony for every "chukka" or goal. A polo match consists of four to six "chukkas", each lasting for 7 minutes of play.

As seen in hockey or basketball, there is lot of potential for the players to commit a foul. For every foul committed, a penalty shot is given to the other team. If the foul has put another player in danger, then the player who committed the foul can be suspended from the match. Players are allowed to try and take an opponent out of the game with a ride-off move. But this needs be done in a way where the other player's safety is not under threat.

The player in the yellow shirt is trying to interrupt the swing of the player in possession of the ball.

All players must wear the normal riding gear that is worn for horse riding. This includes riding boots.

Wall of fame

Argentine polo player Ignacio "Nacho" Figueras is among the top 100 polo players in the world. He is sometimes called the "David Beckham of Polo".

Mexican polo player Carlos Gracida was considered to be a living legend. He became a 10-goal handicap at the age of 25.

Adolfo Cambiaso from Argentina is regarded as one of the best the best players in the world.

Fact card

- In 910 CE, Emperor A-pao-chi of China, ordered all surviving polo players to be beheaded after one of his favourite relatives died in a game of polo.
- Though the game had been mentioned in Sir Anthony Sherley's Travels to Persia (1613), the British tea planters in Assam were the first Europeans to play polo. They only took up the sport in 1859 at Silchar more than two and a half centuries later.
- The USA won the Westchester Cup for the first time in 1909. The cup was contested nine additional times but the USA won it every time except in 1914.

Jumping

There is a certain height above a hurdle that a horse needs to reach while making the jump.

In this sport, the horses are judged on the basis of their strength, speed and agility. The technique of jumping and the rider's contribution to it are both taken into account in this sport.

Origin

Horse jumping competitions came into existence when people began to use their horses to jump over fences. The Inclosure Act which came into force in the eighteenth century allowed people to build fences over their properties. Due to this people who chased fox hounds had to train their horses to jump over fences. Soon, this developed into a competition.

Previously, riders used a deeper saddle with long stirrups for this sport. However, this saddle not only affected the safety and protection of the rider, but also restricted the horse's ability to jump to its fullest capacity.

Captain Federico Caprilli, an Italian cavalry instructor, came up with the concept of a shorter stirrup and a forward positioned saddle. This revolutionised the sport of horse jumping and since then, this type of saddle has been used for jumping.

The rules have changed over time as different national federations had different rules. Now, the Fédération Équestre Internationale (FEI) is the international governing body of this sport.

Short and long hurdles are placed for the horses to jump over.

Riders wear riding helmets to protect their heads in case of a fall from the horse's back.

Rules

According to the FEI, there are jumping penalties for refusal and knockdowns.

- **Refusal:** A refusal is when the horse refuses to follow the rider's command. It costs the rider four faults. While performing a combination of jumps, if a refusal occurs, the entire combination has to be repeated. If the property gets damaged during this and the timer has to be stopped in order to rearrange the setup, the rider may receive an additional penalty on top of the four faults.
- **Knockdowns:** While jumping the fence, if the horse ends up knocking down one of the bars and if it affects the height of the jump, then the rider receives four faults. However, if the knockdown does not affect the jump, then no fault points are given.
- **Time penalties:** The time allotted to perform a combination of jumps depends on the length of the course.

The score is added up at the end of the competition and the player with the highest score wins. There are many other criteria taken into consideration for the final score.

Cross Country

At an international level, cross country equestrian jumping is one leg of a three-part sporting event which is in place to test the endurance of the animal.

All riders wear helmets to prevent injuries in case of a fall from the horse.

Origin

Originally, cross country equestrian jumping was a part of a "long format" endurance event. It had four phases: A, B, C and D. In Phase A, riders carry out a warm-up session on the roads or tracks to loosen up the horse as well as the rider. In Phase B, riders performed a steeplechase where the horse runs 38 kmph and makes seven to eight jumps. Phase C is another road and track session meant to help the horse rest before starting Phase D. This was the cross country race session.

Rules

The cross country course is approximately 4.4–6.5 km long. Riders have to cross about 24–36 solid obstacles. These are built in such a way that they look natural and hence do not upset the horses. However, there are some obstacles that are built to look unnatural to test the horse's bravery.

All obstacles are flagged with a red flag on the right and a white flag on the left side. These obstacles are compulsory and must be attempted. Some obstacles are marked with a black line. These obstacles are not compulsory and the rider may choose another track to avoid them. The rider with the minimum penalty points wins the game. The system of fault points is the same as in the horse jumping sport.

A horse gallops along the track with its rider on the back. Riders are also called "jockeys".

Disobedience from the horse, errors on the course, fall of the rider or horse, fault points and taking too much time to complete the race are some of the reasons for the rider and the horse to be eliminated from the game.

The other reasons that can lead to elimination include:

- The rider is without a proper headgear or seat harness.
- The saddlery is not up to the standards.
- A rider has overtaken another rider, risking his safety.
- A rider deliberately obstructs another rider who is overtaking him/her.
- A rider ignores the signal to stop.
- The horse's head or shoulders are seen outside the flag.

Cross country racing is done on a range of different terrains.

Rodeo

The sport of rodeo developed from a method of herding cattle, which was popular in countries like the USA, Canada, Spain and Mexico. Rodeo tested the skills that cowboys developed while herding cattle.

Origin

Rodeo became a way of life in western USA, western Canada and northern Mexico. The word "rodeo" originates from the Spanish word "rodear", which means to "go around", or "to surround". The word was also used to denote skills of horsemen in the working rodeo.

The cowboy tradition of the USA and Canada adopted the latter usage. Early rodeo-like events of the 1820s and 1830s were conducted in informal settings. It was here that cowboys would gather and go about testing their work skills against each other.

Between 1890 and 1910, rodeo became a topic of public interest, and people realised that it would make a good spectator sport for the entertainment of a large audience. These rodeos were hosted in the Wild West shows that would be conducted in parts of the USA, Canada and Mexico. However, there were no standard set of rules for the events of a rodeo competition until 1929, when associations were formed for the governing and regulation of the rodeo.

The oldest and largest sanctioning body of this event is the Professional Rodeo Cowboys Association (PRCA), which governs about a third of all rodeos staged in the USA.

Riders can compete in roping, team roping, calf roping and barrel racing competitions while mounted on a horse.

There are also saddle bronc riding sports where the rider tries to remain mounted on an aggressive horse.

The saddle used is the regular saddle. The riders might choose to put on a saddle blanket for comfort.

As seen in dressage or polo, the rider cannot put metal or any gear on the hooves of the horse.

Gameplay

The various events held at a rodeo are as follows:

Timed events

Here, a cowboy is trying to throw a lasso around a calf. This sport developed from herding techniques.

- **Roping:** It refers to the roping of a calf or steer. The cowboy must throw a rope tied to the saddle horn with string and a flag. Another version is team roping. In this, there are two cowboys. The first, known as the header ropes the head of the animal. The other cowboy known as the heeler, ropes the legs of the cattle. They both are required to bring the cattle under control, to win the game.
- **Barrel racing:** It is a timed speed and agility event. The horse and the rider gallop around a clover leaf pattern of barrels while making agile turns without knocking the barrels over. The rider who finishes the race first, wins.
- **Steer wrestling:** The rider jumps off his horse onto a Corriente steer and 'wrestles' it to the ground by grabbing it by the horns.
- **Saddle Bronc riding:** Here, a rider sits on a bucking bronc. His/her challenge is to stay on the horse for a stipulated time. The bronc might be barebacked or might have a saddle. The rider can use a single rope to control the bronc. If the bronc is saddled, he/she can use a special saddle without a horn.
- **Bull riding:** It is an event where the cowboys ride full-grown bulls instead of horses. This is way more dangerous as bulls have a tendency to gore and trample fallen riders.

One of the events of a rodeo sport competition is bull riding. In this competition, a rider sits on a large bull and tries to remain mounted while the bull attempts to throw the rider off.

Other activities

Rodeos usually have grand entrance parades and renditions of the Star Spangled Banner. Occasionally, a rodeo queen may be named. There is a fair amount of pageantry here.

Wall of fame

Ty Murray is a professional rodeo star. As one of the most accomplished rodeo athletes, he was often called the "King of Cowboys". He has won the All-Around World Championship title seven times.

Lane Frost was a professional bull rider and rodeo star. He rode for the Professional Rodeo Cowboys Association (PRCA).

Fact card

- It is a myth that a bucking horse is a wild, terrified animal. Several bucking horses are actually riding horses that learned to buck off their riders. Others come from specifically bred wild or bucking stock. The pedigree of bucking is in fact quite valuable and fetches a fair price.
- Rodeos have multiple non-traditional rodeo events that operate outside the rules of sanctioning organisations. These are usually amateur events, such as mutton busting, calf dressing, wild cow milking, calf riding and chuckwagon racing.
- Animal rights activists and groups cite rodeo events as a major source of animal abuse. There have been active protests held at rodeo events against the use of animals. A regular check of the animals and techniques is conducted every year.

Harness Racing

Harness racing is a horse racing sport in which horses trot or pace along the path. The riders sit on a sulky, which is a two-wheeled cart. This cart is pulled by the horses. This sport evolved from the chariot races that took place in ancient civilisations.

The art of the ancient civilisation depicts people using chariots.

Origin

The earliest known records of horse racing date back to Assyria. The Assyrian kings of 1500 BCE maintained elaborate stables. Professional horse trainers used to draw chariots.

Homer's Iliad has several mentions of chariot races. The ancient Olympics of the seventh century BCE had four horse races with two horse races having gone obsolete by then. Locally bred horses were used for this competition, along with those from Asia Minor and Africa.

Chariot racing came into great prominence as a sport after its transfer to Rome. In the first century BCE, Circus Maximus was built. It was a perfect site for chariot racing. By the fourth century CE, hippodrome stands could hold about 200,000 spectators.

Trotting races started in 1554 in the Netherlands. The Golden Whip was first run in 1777 at Soestdijk. This is currently Holland's most famous trotting event.

Harness racing spread rapidly after it was introduced to France in 1836. By the end of the nineteenth century, trotting was prevalent in many parts of Europe including France, Austria and Italy (except Britain).

The races are restricted to certain breeds of horses. In North America, only standardbred horses are used.

Riders are called "drivers". Their use of the whip is limited.

The horses are sometimes harnessed. They need plenty of exercise and practice before racing.

For practice, drivers use a bigger and heavier version of the sulky.

Horses can trot or pace at a set gait. They cannot speed up into a run as this will be against the rules. Disobedience from the horse also affects the race.

The sulky is a light cart equipped with two bicycle wheels. It does not put too much pressure on the horse.

Gameplay & Gear

The modern harness racing vehicle was developed from a single-seat pleasure conveyance. It resembles a U-shaped shaft mounted on two wheels with a seat at the end of the U. While originally weighing in at 56 kg, it had been reduced to 21 kg by 1870.

Races can be conducted in two differing gaits, trotting and pacing. Trotters use diagonal pairs (right front and left hind, then left front and right hind striking the ground simultaneously). Pacers on the other hand move their legs laterally (right front and right hind together, then left front and left hind).

Most harness races begin from behind a motorised starting gate. The horses line up behind a slow vehicle that leads them to the starting line. The vehicle has a winged starting gate that holds the horses. At the starting line, the gates fold away and the vehicles leave. This marks the beginning of the race. The standing start is also used. It is very similar to the one used in flat racing.

When horses pace, they move faster and maintain their pace. In pacing races, horses wear hobbles. Hobbles are straps which connect the legs of the sulky with the horse's sides. This is why they rarely break stride. However, the pace is not affected by the hobbles. The pace of the horses is a normal, natural gait that they follow. The hobbles just allow them to move as quickly as possible.

Wall of fame

The Standardbred is a popular horse breed from the USA. It is the most preferred horse in harness racing. The first Standardbred horse can be traced back to the eighteenth century. They are also used for pleasure riding and for display in horse shows.

The first French Trotter came to be in the nineteenth century from the Norman breed of horses. It has English Thoroughbred and Norfolk Trotter blood. These horses are used for harness racing in European countries.

The Orlov Trotter is one of the most famous Russian horses used for harness racing.

All these horses are wearing hobbles. The rider sets the pace initially and only seeks to maintain that pace through the race.

Fact card

- "Messenger" is the horse which was the founding sire of the Standardbred horse. It was a gray Thoroughbred horse brought to the USA in 1788. Hambletonian 10 was the great-grandson of this horse. He gained a wide following for his racing prowess.
- Most drivers use whips to lightly hit the horses and control their pace. All countries have strict rules about the use of the whip and its restrictions. Norway has banned the whip entirely.

Equestrian Vaulting

Equestrian vaulting is a sport that combines the discipline, skill and grace of gymnastics with the strength and control of horse riding.

Origin

It is said that the sport originated some time during the ancient Roman games. Acrobats used to display their skills on horses while they cantered around. However, the other theory about its origin claims that it was invented in ancient Crete where bull leaping was a common activity. Regardless, it is confirmed that people have been performing acrobatic and dance-like movements on the backs of moving horses and cattle for over 2,500 years.

The present name of the sport comes from the French phrase "la voltige". Modern vaulting developed in post-war Germany. The intention was to introduce children to equestrian sports. Today, vaulting is open to both men and women. The International Federation for Equestrian Sports, officially known as the Fédération Équestre Internationale (FEI), recognises equestrian vaulting as one of the 10 equestrian disciplines.

Today, vaulting is most popular in Europe and North America. In 1986, the first FEI World Vaulting Championship was held in Bulle, Switzerland. Since the World Equestrian Games of 1990 in Stockholm, vaulting has been included in every edition of the event.

This is the flag move. It is a compulsory move performed by all individual participants. Here, the rider hops onto the knees and extends the opposite hand and leg. Then, the rider changes position and performs the same move using the other hand and leg. The rider should hold the move for four strides.

Here, the riders are attempting a jump and switch move.

The position of the hands and legs needs to be proper. Holding them loose or bending the hands when they should be straight, leads to the deduction of points.

Riders can also attempt to carry each other or switch seats.

The legs must be held stiff and the rider must be in control at all times.

Gameplay

Competitive vaulting can be divided into the following categories on the basis of participation: individuals, pairs (pas-de-deux) and teams. Beginners compete at a trot while more advanced participants compete at a canter.

The vaulting horse moves in a 15-m circle and is directed by a lunger (or "longeur" in French) who stands in the centre.

This is an individual freestyle move. This participant is attempting a position called the "mill", where the legs alternate in this position for four strides.

Horses wear a roller and a thick back pad. The rider performs some stunts using the special handles attached to the roller.

Vaulting competitions consist of some compulsory exercises and some choreographed freestyle exercises. The latter are performed to a musical score. Each exercise is scored on a scale of 0 to 10. Even the horse is judged on how it moves and behaves. Mount, basic seat, flag, mill, scissors, stand and flank are the seven compulsory exercises that must be performed by all participants.

Freestyle events were originally called a "kur". For individual participants, the kur is a one-minute freestyle round. For teams, the kur lasts for four minutes.

Standing, kneeling, mounting and dismounting, handstands, and aerial moves like jumps, leaps and tumbles are all a part of the freestyle vaulting routine. Some of the more complex moves mentioned here can only be seen at the highest levels of the sport. A child or beginner will more likely perform variations on simple kneels and planks.

Horses used for vaulting do not wear saddles. They have a surcingle (or a roller) and a thick back pad. There are special handles on the surcingle to help the vaulter. There are also leather loops called "cossack stirrups".

The FEI regulates dress codes for competitive vaulting. Guidelines are revised every two to three years. They generally adhere to the tenet that "vaulters must wear form-fitting uniforms that do not conceal the line and form of the vaulter's body, and must not hinder the movement of the vaulter or the safe interaction between the vaulters". Accessories like belts, capes or hats are prohibited for this reason.

This participant is practicing a handstand on the back of his horse. He must hold the pose for one entire minute.

Wall of fame

An individual freestyle vaulter performing the first part of the famous scissor move in Germany.

Team vaulting is one of the most famous forms of this sport as teams perform freestyle moves to balance, jump, throw and lift the members.

Annelobke Van Dijk, Marijke Dikkens and Sofie Jackson performing the popular throw and lift move in the team freestyle competition.

Fact card

- Vaulting is used as a therapeutic exercise in some instances. People with disabilities often benefit from interacting with the horse and, if they are doing it in teams, interacting with their team members. They are encouraged to perform simple movements with the help of "spotters".
- Vaulting has a history as an equestrian act at circuses where it was often performed along with trapeze events.

Buzkashi

Buzkashi is also called "Kokpar". Buzkashi is a Persian word which literally translates to "goat grabbing". It is a sport that developed in Central Asia.

Origin

Buzkashi is the national game of Afghanistan. It may have begun with the nomadic Turkic-Mongol people. Today, several Central Asian ethnic groups indigenously share buzkashi.

In this sport, players race their horses and try to drag the carcass of a goat or calf to the goal post. This sport was banned under the Taliban regime. But today, it is the national sport of Afghanistan. Earlier, a match would last for days.

Rules

Buzkashi was a fierce and barbaric game where there were really no rules. Initially, it was only a matter of etiquette to not harm your fellow rider intentionally by pushing him off the horse or by whipping him. However, now there are well-formulated rules, both in terms of equipment and play.

The carcass is usually headless. There are two forms to this sport. In one form, the carcass is picked up and moved in any direction. The game ends when the player reaches a point clear of all other players.

Fact card

- In Tajikistan, this sport is played as a tournament, which starts in November and ends in April. If the temperature is too high, the match is postponed.
- The American film, Rambo III features a game of Buzkashi.
- In the twentieth century, during the Soviet occupation of Afghanistan, the use of discarded Soviet Helmets and military boots as gear was common.

In one form of the game, the players need to drag the carcass around a flag and then throw the carcass into a scoring circle made on the ground.

The ground has a square layout. Each side is 400-m long. Each team consists of 10 riders. Of these, only four riders from each team can play on the field at the same time. In Afghanistan, the team has 10 players but only five riders can play in one-half of the match.

Each match lasts for 90 minutes. The match is split into two halves of 45 minutes. There is only one 15-minute break between the two halves.

The game is supervised by a referee. A rider can only be substituted in the game based on the decision taken by the referee.

The big goals are called the "kazans". These are made on the ground with a diameter of 3.6 m and height of 1.5 m. They are placed on the opposite sides of the field.

A point is scored each time a kokpar (goat carcass) is placed in an opponent's kazan. A "kokboru" is brought to the centre of the field after scoring a goal.

This is a spectator sport. Keeping in mind the safety of the spectators, the riders are not allowed to move or ride towards them. They cannot take the help of a spectator to play. Players take an oath at the beginning of the match to play justly.

In Tajikistan, dozens of players can compete against each other at one time. There are several safety measures adopted to avoid accidents.

Campdrafting

Campdrafting, a unique equestrian sport, is turning into a fast-growing horse sport in Australia. This popular sport involves a rider and horse working cattle. Campdrafting, like the rodeo was developed as a method for cowboys to show off their skills at their job.

Origin

This sport was invented in outback Queensland. It started as a contest between the stockmen and the drovers to prove their horse skills to each other. They held informal competitions. The first of such informal competitions was held in Tenterfield in 1885 at the Tenterfield Show Society. It was the first formal campdrafting competition on record. A man named Clarence Smith created the rules and judging procedures for the game.

Each year at the Warwick Gold Cup, held over six days, as many as 1800 campdrafters compete for prize money. This is one of the premier events in campdrafting in Australia and reflects the popularity of the game. Paradise Lagoons in Queensland is the venue of the richest campdraft in Australia. The prize money for the competition is 230,000 Australian dollars, which is distributed over four days of the competition.

Rules

The perfect horse for campdrafting should be about 15 hands. It also needs to be agile enough to easily take a beast from the camp. Australian Stock Horses are usually used in campdrafting.

To start with, the rider on the horseback, must "cut out" one beast from the mob of cattle in the yard or the "camp". He must then block and turn the beast at least two or three times, to prove to the judge that he has the beast under control. Then, he needs to take it out of the yard using right and left hand turns in a figure eight. Finally, the rider must guide the cattle through two pegs, known as "the gate". This is an outside course. It must be completed in 40 seconds.

The rider is attempting to steer the cattle in the direction of the gate.

The horse might need to use pressure and strength to push a bullock around to the correct position. The horse must be quick enough to control the bullock. The horse should be obedient and willing to comply with the instructions of the rider. He should also be familiar with the cattle. If these conditions are not met, a horse cannot be allowed in the competition as this might put the rider, the horse and the cattle in danger. Most Australian Stock Horses are bred and trained for these competitions from a young age.

Motorbike campdrafting follows the same pattern but replaces horses with motorbikes.

Fact card

- In some parts of Australia, people practice "open campdrafting". This is when certain beasts are selected and drafted from the mob of cattle while they are still in their paddock, instead of droving the cattle for yard drafting.
- In 2007 and 2008, the equine influenza affected so many animals that several drafting events had to be cancelled.

Endurance Riding

Along with speed, another important attribute of a horse is its endurance. Horses are often bred for long-distance travel. Endurance riding is a modern form of the military practice of taking horses on long runs.

Endurance races can be competed for distances of 80 km or 160 km. It can also be a one-day event.

Origin

Endurance riding was developed as an organised activity in the USA after World War II. It was based on the Polish and Russian cavalries used in World War I.

Endurance racing as a formal sport began in 1955. This was when Wendell Robie, an American citizen, and a group of equestrians rode from the Lake Tahoe area across the Sierra Nevada Range to Auburn in less than 24 hours. Endurance racing was first brought to Europe in the 1960s. It is regulated by the FEI and also the regulating bodies in Europe and the USA.

A rider moves the horse along the trail. Horses are usually not saddled and wear light equipment.

Fact card

- Wendell Robie followed the historic Western States Trail. Today, this trail is known as the Tevis Cup. It remains the most difficult of any 160-km ride in the world because of the severe terrain, high altitude and high temperatures.
- Arabian horses are the dominant breed as they are naturally selected for their speed and stamina by breeders from all walks of life.

Rules

In the USA, the American Endurance Ride Conference (AERC) sanctions endurance rides. In the UK, Endurance GB is the governing body for the sport.

A veterinarian inspects the horses to ensure that they are fit to perform in the ride before the race begins. The ride is divided into sections with different names (legs, phases, etc.), depending on the sanctioning organisation. The horses are stopped for a veterinary inspection after each phase. These are also known as vetgates.

There is an enforced rest period of around 25-40 minutes to feed, water and cool-off the horses after each race that they partake in.

The first rider to cross the finish line with a clean bill of health at each check point is the winner.

There are tests to check the speed and recovery rate of the horse. If the horse is pushed beyond its limit, the rider is given a penalty. The competitions, usually, also award those participants whose horses finished in the top 10 for 80-km distances or more. In some cases, there is a Best Conditioned Horse award. It is considered to be more important than the first place. Its prize money is also higher.

Horseball

Horseball is a unique horse-riding game, which involves the use of a ball. It is a team sport where points are awarded when a team manages to shoot a ball through a hoop with a diameter of 1-m.

Origin

Horseball comes from Argentina. It is a combination of polo, basketball and rugby. An old sport called "pato" was played in Argentina. Pato originated in Argentina in the early 1700s, but was soon outlawed due to high mortality rates among players. Also, the name "pato" derives from the fact that the original game used a live duck. Eventually, the live duck was replaced by a ball and in 1953, the Federacion Argentina de Pato declared it to be the Argentinian national sport.

Today, horseball is one of the 10 disciplines officially recognised by the International Federation for Equestrian Sports. The International Horseball Federation has 18 members, including eight outside Europe: Algeria, Argentina, Australia, Brazil, Canada, China, Kyrgyzstan and Mexico.

The hoop has a net attached so that the ball doesn't suddenly drop from the hoop onto a horse standing close by.

Rules

Each team has four players along with two substitutes. The players need to make a minimum of three passes between three different players of their team. They must then lob the ball through a vertical hoop goal, thus scoring a point.

A match begins with a pickup. The first pickup requires a horse to be cantering. The opposing team can defend the move by preventing them from being able to score. Pushing opponents out of the playing area using their horse's weight or getting alongside a player and grabbing the ball from the attacker, are the preferred defense tactics.

Players must not leave the saddle during a grab. If a player leaves the saddle, they will give away a penalty. The grab may not go on for longer than three seconds or the attacker gives away a penalty.

Riders wear helmets to protect their heads during a game. The reason for high mortality rates in the past was that the riders would fall off their horses during a game.

The ball used in this game is attached to six different handles. This is so that the horses can pick up the ball with their teeth.

Players pass the ball by throwing it to their team members. They must practice how to handle the ball with its six handles.

Fact card

- When the ball is dropped or falls to the ground, anyone can pick it up. However, they must be travelling in the same direction to prevent a collision.
- The game is played on a soft, non-slip surface like sand.

Horse Racing

People have been racing horses since ancient times. Horse breeders are always in search of a breed that can run faster, is stronger and has greater endurance. Horse racing developed from the practice of determining a horse's value by pitting it against another horse.

Origin

Archaeological records reveal that horse racing as a sport, emerged a long time ago in Ancient Greece, Babylon, Syria and Egypt. There are also important mythological occurrences of horse racing, such as the contest between the steeds of Odin and the giant Hrungnir in Norse mythology. Historically, equestrians honed their skills through games and races. As a result, racing honed necessary martial skills. Equestrian sports provided entertainment for crowds.

Horse racing mainly evolved from impromptu competitions between riders or jockeys. The horses and their riders needed special skills. This requirement led to the systematic development of special breeds of horses. Also, special equipment was developed to practice this sport safely.

This has fortunately led to the preservation of riding skills that would otherwise have been lost.

Presumably, organised racing began in countries like China, Persia, Arabia, and other countries of the Middle East and in North Africa, where horsemanship became one of the most highly developed skills. These cultures are responsible for the development of Arabian, Barb and Turk horses that contributed so much to the field of early European racing. Europe was familiarised with these breeds as a result of the crusades that brought them in contact with the Middle East. Racing in medieval England began when professional riders rode horses for sale in competition to display the horse's speed to buyers.

The beginning of the modern era of racing is generally considered to have been the inauguration of the English classic races, the St Leger in 1776, the Oaks in 1779 and the Derby in 1780.

Rules

Different races have different rules. The basic rules state that jockeys may not commit a foul or hit each other. It is considered illegal to cross over into another lane in a manner that would endanger other horses. Other than that, players must not take-off before the starter's gun.

The different races are segregated based on distance and track. Some of the most famous ones are:

In Britain	In North America
2,000 Guineas Stakes	Kentucky Derby
1,000 Guineas Stakes	Breeders' Cup Classic
Epsom Oaks	
Epsom Derby	

In this picture, two jockeys are racing against each other on their horses.

The most famous horses in recent history have been given the "Horse of the Year" award. This award is given out once every year.

Some of the winners are:

2016 – California Chrome
2015 – American Pharoah
2013 – Wise Dan

The horses must cross certain obstacles in the race track by jumping or galloping over them.

Wall of fame

Calvin Borel is an American thoroughbred horse racer. He has won several races, but his win at the 2009 Kentucky Derby was the most memorable one.

Frankie Dettori is a British jockey who has won the title of "Champion Jockey" three times.

Julie Krone is the first woman jockey to have won a Triple Crown race. She also made the Cowgirl Hall of Fame.

Fact card

- In Norse Mythology, Odin rode an eight-legged horse called Sleipnir that was faster than an eye-blink.
- Animal rights groups vehemently protest thoroughbred racing. Most thoroughbreds are three years old and their lives are drastically shortened by the stress of racing at such a young age.
- Different breeds of horses have been developed, that excel in each of the specific disciplines. The ones that are most suited to this sport are the Thoroughbred, Quarter Horse, Arabian, Paint and Appaloosa. The Thoroughbred is the most dominant of these.

Pato

Pato is the traditional game of Argentina which has gone from being a bizarre sport to a very mainstream sport. The first version of this game was so violent that several groups of people were offended by its existence. But in its refined and modern form, the sport has become very popular. It is similar to horseball in its gameplay.

Origin

Accounts of early versions of pato have been written since 1610. It was originally played in the area between two neighbouring ranches known as "estancias".

"Pato" is the Spanish word for "duck". In the earlier version of the sport, a live duck was used in the place of a ball. It was put inside a basket. The game is also called "juego del pato", which translates to "the duck game".

Pato was a violent game and was banned multiple times. Many players were trampled underfoot. Some even lost their lives in the knife fights that took place in the heat of the game.

Pato was regulated through the efforts of the ranch owner Alberto del Castillo Posse, in the 1930s. He drafted a set of rules which were inspired by modern polo.

With the use of a ball, the sport became socially acceptable. In 1953, President Juan Perón declared pato as Argentina's national game.

The ring used in Pato looks similar to the ring used in horseball, as the latter game was developed from pato.

Gameplay

In modern pato, two four-member teams fight for possession of a ball. The ball has six conveniently sized handles. A point is scored by throwing the ball through a basket with a vertical rim. The diameter of the rings is 100 cm. It is placed atop 240 cm high poles. The net that holds the ball after a goal is closed and extends for 140 cm.

Pato is played for six 8-minute periods. When in possession, the player must extend his arm holding the pato to allow others a chance to grab it. Players can tug at the pato to relieve possession.

During the tug itself, or cinchada, both players must stand on the stirrups and avoid sitting on the saddle, while the hand not involved in tugging must hold the reins.

The defending team is not allowed to move in the direct path of a player.

Team members throw the six-handled ball into the net from close quarters.

As seen in other ball sports, team members are assigned numbers to their jerseys.

Fact card

- If a player does not extend his/her arm while holding the ball, it is termed a "negada" or refusal.
- Since over 90 per cent of the people of Argentina have not seen a game of pato, football may soon replace it as the national game.

Tent Pegging

Tent pegging is a sport that involves the use of a lance to pierce and pick up a ring or a small piece of paper from the ground. An additional handicap is the fact that it is played from the back of a galloping horse.

A rider uses the lance to pierce the ground target set.

Origin

The competitive sport of tent pegging evolved out of cavalry training exercises designed to develop the cavaliers' prowess with the sword and lance from horseback. Cavaliers have practised this game since the fourth century BCE. It was first seen in ancient Asian empires and later spread to European empires. Hence, the exact origins of this sport are not yet clear. The International Equestrian Federation states that most equestrian authorities believe that tent pegging began in India in the Middle Ages. It was a tactic used on the battlefields by cavalry on horseback against the elephant-mounted troops.

Gameplay

The Olympics Council of Asia included tent pegging as an official sport in 1982, and the International Federation for Equestrian Sports recognised it as an official equestrian discipline in 2004.

Tent pegging involves a mounted horseman riding full tilt at a small target. He then pierces or cuts it using a sword or lance and carries it away.

Usually, players play without gloves as it spoils the grip on the wooden stick.

Players can use a lance or sword depending on the event and the competition rules.

The end of the lance is used to pierce, pick up and carry the ground target.

The umbrella term also includes games such as:

- **Ring jousting** - a rider attempts to pass the tip of his weapon through a ring that is suspended while he is galloping.
- **Lemon sticking** - the rider tries to stab or slice a lemon suspended from a cord, or sitting on a platform.
- **Quintain tilting** - the rider charges a mannequin mounted on a swivelling or rocking pedestal.

Fact card

- The Indian Army's 61st Cavalry regiment is the last and only horse mounted cavalry regiment in the world. As a result, the Indian Army is one of the leading champions in tent pegging at a global level.

Polocrosse

This is a team sport which combines the games of polo and lacrosse into a fun activity.

Origin

Two instructors at the National School of Equitation at Kingston Vale near London had developed an exercise to supplement the work at the riding school. This exercise aimed to help young riders take better charge of their horses.

In 1938, Mr and Mrs Edward Hirst of Sydney found an article, in an English Horse Magazine, about polocrosse. They visited the school in England and saw the sport. It was being played indoors at that time. They returned to Australia with sticks, balls and rulebooks to adapt the game as an outdoor sport.

Alf Pitty, a well-known horseman and polo player, helped in giving the first recorded polocrosse demonstration at the Ingleburn Sports Ground near Sydney in 1939.

The final game used only one horse and could be played by players of any age.

Polocrosse is played outdoors on a field or pitch. Polocrosse is also seen as a practice sport to improve riding skills.

Fact card

- The stick and ball can only be carried in the player's dominant hand. They are allowed to catch the ball on the opposite side but must bring it back to the dominant immediately. Failure to do this or crossing the stick across the horse otherwise is a foul.

The rules of blocking and possession of horseball apply to this sport.

Gameplay

Each polocrosse rider uses a cane or fibreglass stick which has a racquet head with a loose thread net at its end. A four-inch soft sponge ball is supposed to be carried into the net.

The objective is to score goals by passing the ball through the opposing team's goal posts. All players must use a safety helmet, racquet, ball, leg wraps and coronet boots for the horse.

Each team consists of six players. Each player plays either two, three or four chukkas of six to eight minutes.

The team is divided into two or three sections. They play on-field or off-field depending on the rules of the game. Every match has either four, six or eight chukkas, so three players in each section play the position of a No. 1, attack, a No. 2, midfield or a No. 3, defence.

A player must pick up a ball with the racquet, hold it in it and then ride with it. Until the No. 1 has possession of the ball in the goal scoring area, the players keep passing the ball between themselves by throwing it. They cannot take the ball over the penalty line to score.

MIND SPORTS

"Mind over matter" is a common saying that we've all heard. The sports we have read about so far place a lot of importance on physical dexterity, coordination, stamina and skill. But what about mental dexterity and agility?

A "mind sport" is defined as any sport that puts focus on the use of mental skills and talent rather than any physical component. As a result, what constitutes a mental sport and what does not, is a matter of some mental debate. Most mind sports use a prop of some sort like a board or cards. Chess, monopoly and poker are the most common examples of these types of mind sports. However, certain mind sports are purely based on mental capacity. Examples of these are commonly seen in the form of speed-reading or memory games.

There are also some who may classify sports that involve technical skills, such as computer coding or programming as mind sports. Mind sports are varied in nature. Winning a mind sport might revolve around strategy, planning or pure mental discipline. Let us take a look at some mind sports and understand what they are all about!

Did you know? "Mind sports" was used as a term for the first time during the 1997 Mind Sports Olympiad. It is taken to be the Olympics of mind sports. Tony Buzan also used this term to describe the game of backgammon in 1996.

Chess

Chess is a two-player game. It is one of the oldest and toughest mind sports known to us. Millions of people around the world play chess every day. It is a strategic game that follows a monarchy and war scenario.

Chess board: Traditionally made of wood, the board has squares in rows and columns. The squares have light and dark colours alternatively. The first two rows from each horizontal end have the player's pieces.

Origin

The game originated in India and dates back to sixth century AD. There are some connects of it in Ancient China. From India, it spread to Persia when the Persian rulers travelled there. It then moved to Arab kingdoms and their conquests. It spread to faraway empires because at the time, colonial and imperial powers were fighting for control over one another. The golden era of chess was in 1886, when the first World Chess Championship was held.

Equipment

The equipment includes a chess board with squares setup in eight rows and eight columns. There are two sets of game pieces. Traditionally, one set is white while the other is black. The players choose one set and are referred to as "White" or "Black", based on the set they choose.

Various forms of this game are practiced, but the most famous is the original visible board based game with no time limit. There is a "fast chess" variation which requires a player to take decisions quickly as the timer ticks on and they make their move. The rules for that are set differently; the primary rules remain the same. Each piece has its own characteristic feature in the game. The pieces have to be set up according to the rules.

Rook: The rook can only move in straight line blocks and side line blocks. It cannot kill or move diagonally.

Queen: The queen is placed between the king and the bishop. The queen can move in all directions both forward and backward. It is the most useful piece in the game.

Bishop: The bishop is placed beside the knight at the back of the board. It can only move diagonally on the board.

Pawn: The pawn can move only one block at a time and only in the forward direction. It can kill any piece on the board that is ahead and diagonal to it.

Pawn: It has a special ability to move two blocks in its first move on the board. In some cases, if a pawn reaches the end of the board into the other player's territory, it can be promoted into any character on the board except the king.

War elephant or rook: It is placed at the corner of the board at the start of the game. It has a special ability of "castling" with the king. In this move, the bishop and knight move out from their squares. The king can then exchange places with the elephant in order to safeguard its position. But, in the process, they both have to take one block ahead. So, the king is in the knight's block and the elephant in the bishop's block.

Knight: It has the ability to jump over other pieces on the board in order to reach its destined block. With this ability, the knight can kill a piece even if it has another piece blocking it. It is placed beside the elephant at the start of the game.

Bishop: It can move in any direction diagonally, both forward and backwards.

Queen: It is the most powerful piece and should be used wisely. It moves like the bishop and rook combined.

King: If the player's king is in danger, he/she will have no option but to move it to safety at the cost of any other piece, including the queen. A threat to the opponent's king piece is marked by bringing a piece close to it, in a killing position. The person must then say "CHECK". A situation where there is no movement possible for the king and it is under threat at all possible blocks, is known as "CHECKMATE". With this, the game is over. Another way of ending the game would be to reach a stale mate where there are few pieces left on the board but too many possible movements.

Knight:
The knight can move three blocks at one time. The twist is that its move is shaped like an L. It can jump over pieces of either colour.

King:
The king is the most important piece. It can move only one step in any direction. If the king is killed, the game is lost.

Wall of fame

From 1985 until his retirement, Garry Kasparov remained the #1 World Chess Champion. He is considered to be the greatest chess player of all time.

Emanuel Lasker from Germany held the position of the World Chess Champion for 27 years, from 1894 to 1921.

Viswanathan Anand was the undisputed World Chess Champion in 2000, 2007,2008, 2010 and 2012.

Fact card

- The longest game of chess theoretically possible is with 5,949 moves.
- The first folding chessboard was made by a priest, who was not allowed to play chess. He made it so that it could look like a book after it was folded.
- The word "checkmate" comes from the Persian word "Shah Mat". It is a dramatic word and translates to "the king is dead". It is no wonder that this phrase is used once all defence for the king is lost.

Draughts

Draughts is an exciting board game that has been played for centuries. It involves only one kind of piece on each side and is considered by many to be a simplified version of chess.

The game of draughts might have several rules, but the game simple enough to pick up.

Origin

Draughts originated in Egypt in the sixteenth century. There is some archeological evidence which suggests that the game of draughts could have been invented in 200 BCE, as the excavations have shown evidence of people playing it as far back as then. This game is also called "checkers" in the USA. Its first published mention was made in Valencia, Spain, in 1547.

Gameplay

Draughts is played on an 8 x 8 checkerboard. It has light and dark squares. The pieces can only move on the dark squares. Some versions of draughts are played on 10 × 10 and 12 × 12 boards. One player picks the dark pieces while another picks the light pieces. They take turns to play their moves. The pieces are called "men". One set is called "red" and the other set is called "white". The king is marked with two pieces which are kept one on top of the other.

In the game of Turkish Draughts, both light and dark pieces are used for gameplay.

This is the king row. Once the opponent reaches here, he/she makes his/her piece the "king" piece.

The player with the white pieces goes second, unlike chess, where the player with the white set goes first.

At the start of the game, the 12 men in each set are placed in three rows. The men can only be arranged on the dark squares. The row that is closest to the player is called the "king row".

The player with the dark set makes the first move. The men can move only diagonally on the dark squares. A player can only make one move at one time. If the player sees an opportunity to capture the opponent's piece, he/she can move one of his/her pieces two consecutive steps in the same line. The player jumps over the opponent's piece and lands on the first dark step after it. Then the player takes away the opponent's piece from the board. In one turn, a player can capture several pieces from the opponent, but it should be done in successive jumps with one piece. In such an event, the player can also move in a "zigzag" manner. In this game, a player can touch a piece but decide not to move it.

If a player's piece manages to move to the opponent's king row, then it can become a king. A king has the advantage of moving both forward and backward. The game can end in two ways. Either all of the opponent's pieces are off the board or they are in a state where no further move can be made to capture the pieces.

Fact card

- During World War II, a special deluxe edition of the draughts board was released.
- The game travelled across continents before it reached South America. It is here that it got the name "checkers".

Scrabble

Scrabble was invented in the modern era as a word game. It is fairly popular today and is often used as an educational tool. In this game, the players are given tiles with letters on them. They must make words from these letters.

Players choose from 100 tiles, of which 98 are marked with a letter, and two are blank and carry no points. They can be used as substitutes for other letters.

Origin

Earlier known as "Lexiko", this game originated in the USA and was developed by an architect. In 1948, James Brunot from Connecticut claimed rights and changed the name to "Scrabble" after adding a few features to it. "Scrabble" is a trademark of the Hasbro, Inc. in the USA and Canada. Outside of these countries, it is a trademark of Mattel, Inc.

Rules

The rules of this game changed every few years until finally it was copyrighted. From then on the rules have remained the same. The most common rules are given below.

Words can be played from a pre-existing alphabet on the board. A player has the option of forming parallel words, as long as all the words formed are valid. A player can challenge the word played by another if he/she feels it is not a correct word. The penalty, if this claim is true, is that the player will lose a turn and flush his/her tiles.

A blank tile can be used for any letter needed. There is an option of passing the turn. If there is a tie, then the player who exchanged fewer tiles becomes the winner.

This is a Scrabble board with its pieces. It is a trademark of Hasbro, Inc. and Mattel, Inc.

Each piece has a number (except the blank ones), which indicates how many points the piece is worth.

If a player uses all seven tiles in one turn, it is called a "bingo" move.

At the start of the game, players select the seven tiles from a bag of letters. To play the game of Scrabble, there should be at least two players. Each player chooses an order and sticks to the playing order for the rest of the game.

A player forms a word on the tile and scores himself/herself according to the number on the tiles used. The tiles that were used are replaced by taking out new tiles from the bag. The player cannot see which tiles are being picked. According to the board, there are options of scoring more by landing on special tiles like double letter, triple letter, double word and triple word.

Fact card

- Initially, the game was very tough to sell and no manufacturer would take an order.
- The game comes with a word list. The word list is adapted as per the different age groups that play the game of Scrabble.
- The game is available in different languages. This makes the game more complex for those who are playing the game in their second or third language.

Backgammon

Backgammon is one of the oldest board games known to the humankind. This game of skill and strategy requires two players. Luck is said to play a big part in deciding the winner. As a result, even amateurs are encouraged to compete in the game.

This old backgammon game was recovered from the Vasa, sunk in 1628.

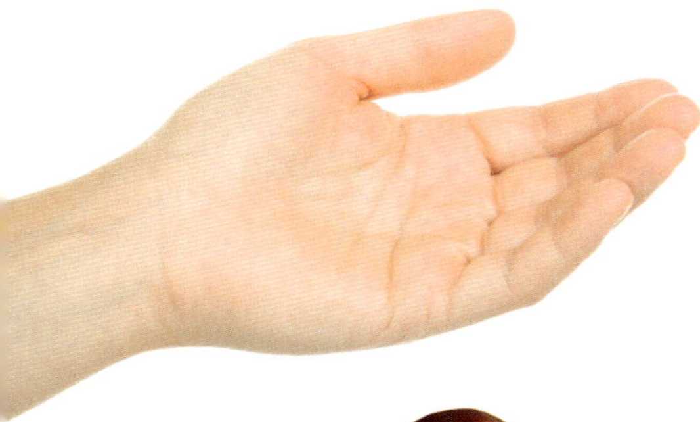

Origin

Backgammon may have originated more than 5000 years ago. It is said to have originated in Mesopotamia. It was played with dice. The dice were made of human bones. Earlier, this game had many names for players of different languages. As the Romans made the game very popular, it was called "deodecum scripta et tabulea".

The rules changed according to the social status of the people playing it. Around the 1920s, the game began losing its appeal because it was difficult to set wagers for the winners. The game would last for a very long time, which was another factor of its declining popularity.

In order to revive the game, the stakes were doubled and a multiplayer version was introduced. This is the backgammon that we play today.

Each die has 2, 4, 16, 32 and 64 on its faces. Players roll the dice to play the game.

Backgammon pieces are called "checkers", "draughts", "men", "stones" and even "counters".

Each side has 12 triangles called "points". Look closely to see the horseshoe the triangles form from the 1st point to the 24th point.

The checkers come in light and dark colours like black and white, as seen in this board.

Traditionally, the backgammon board is made of wood. The board can close with the pieces inside it.

Gameplay

To start the game, players take turns to roll the dice and make a note of their points. The player with the higher number plays first. Players must move the checkers according to the numbers on the dice.

If the dice roll a two and a four, then the player must move two points forward then use another checker, or the same one, to move four points forward.

The objective of the game is to get all the checkers into your own home board. Each die has its own value. The movement of checkers is determined respectively. A player who rolls double on the dice plays a combination that fits him/her the best.

Any time a player has more checkers on the bar, he/she has to enter those checkers into the opposite home board.

After the last checker has been entered, anything that is unused on the dice must be played. Each player gets 15 checkers. Once all of a player's checkers are on the board, he/she must move it into the home board. He/she should also start bearing off the checkers.

This game is played on an agreed per stake point basis. At any point, a player can make an offer of doubling and the other one can refuse as well. But in this process of denial, the player will lose one point. If not, he/she must accept and play for double the stakes as the original.

If the loser has even one checker, he/she loses the equivalent of the value shown on the doubling cube. If the player has not borne off any of his checkers, then he/she loses double the value.

The worse-case scenario here is, when a player has borne off none of his checkers and has one checker on the winner's side of the board. In this case, he/she loses thrice the value of the doubling cube.

Modern backgammon boards use various designs on the board. However, the basic positioning of the checkers and points is the same.

Wall of fame

- Carol Crawford won the World Backgammon Championship Award in 1973. She was the second woman to win this award. Both she and her husband, John Crawford, have made a name for themselves in backgammon.
- John Crawford also loved bridge and was a member of the US team which won the three Bermuda Bowls in 1950, 1951 and 1953. He invented the "Crawford rule" in backgammon which restricts the use of the double cube in a match.
- Akiko Yazawa is a professional backgammon player from Tokyo. She won the World Backgammon Championship in 2014. She ranked 17th in the Giants of Backgammon in 2013, becoming the first female Backgammon Giant.
- Jorge Alberto Pan was an Argentine backgammon player. He won the 32nd World Backgammon Championship in Monte Carlo in 2007.
- Philip Vischjager was a Dutch backgammon player who won the 31st World Championship Backgammon in Monte Carlo.

Fact card

- Plato said that this game represented the movement of the planet and that chess represented war.
- Persians take the checkers used in this game as symbols for days, weeks and hours.
- When the checkers is double the value, it is called "gammon". When the checkers is triple the value, it is called "backgammon".
- When playing with money, a player can "beaver" when offered the cube. It doubles the value of the game but the player has possession of the cube.

Xiangqi

Xiangqi is a Chinese game that is extremely popular. It is played by a number of people in China, Singapore, Vietnam and several other Asian countries. This unique game, also known as "Chinese Chess", involves a lot of strategy. It has rules different from that of "Chess" played in the west. It is a typical army related game.

Origin

According to ancient books, the phrase "Xiangqi" was first mentioned in the fourth century BCE. Several famous Chinese books had mentioned this phrase. The game has changed quite a lot since then. The Northern Song Dynasty made the final amends and put forth the game that we play today.

Equipment

The board is around 9 lines wide and 10 lines long. All pieces are played on the intersections and are called "points". Vertical lines are called "files" and horizontal lines are called "ranks".

There are two square zones that are demarcated by diagonal lines that connect opposite corners. They are known as "Palace" or "Fortress". Regardless of the rules followed in different countries, universally "red" moves first.

The pieces are flat and circular disks. They are labelled and engraved with a Chinese character, each with a meaning.

The board and the meaning behind the squares are such that the board resembles a warpath.

The players choose red or black sets of pieces.

Just like chess, draught, backgammon, scrabble and all the other board games, this game can be played by children and adults alike.

Every movement acquires one point. Alternate movements keep taking place through the course of the game. The pieces cannot move through a point that is already taken up.

A piece can be moved onto an enemy point. Hence, this shows that that piece has been captured and has to be thrown out of the board completely.

The twist comes when the player is allowed to move sideways after he crosses the river with his piece. The cannon piece has a special move for this.

The game simply ends when the other team's general has been captured.

But the threatened position is marked by giving a check to the opposition. In chess, there is an option of stalemate in which the result of the game is considered to be a draw. In this game, if there are no legal moves left for the player, it is considered a loss. The various pieces include—general, horse, elephant, advisor, chariot, cannon and soldier.

Fact card

- In Xiangqi, the battle is usually focussed on one area of the board because of the long-range pieces and the small size of the board.
- "Xiang" means elephants and "Qi" means pieces.

Mahjong

Though Mahjong is a game of skill, strategy and calculation, the luck of the player also plays an important role in it. It is a tile game. It is played both competitively and for recreation. In its simplest form, the player has to match identical tiles.

Origin

The game is compared to the card game of rummy. Mahjong originated in China in 500 BCE. Legend says that it was developed by a philosopher named Confucius. This game was named after a bird that the philosopher was very fond of. It initially started with a pack of 40 paper cards, with numbers from one to nine written on them in different suits. It also had extra flower cards.

As people started losing interest in the game, it underwent several changes in the fourteenth century. It was reborn. Some say that it was played by the Chinese army soldiers to pass time in the 1870s. The game was banned by the government in 1949. The ban was revoked in 1985. Today, it is one of the favourite games for passing time.

In this picture, you can see the players setting up the tiles. There is a short period of shuffling after which the tiles are arranged.

Rules

The rules of this game are simple. Each player picks up a tile from the wall and then discards it by putting it in the centre. There is an option of announcing the tile if the player desires to do so. It goes on until there is a legal winning hand. Then the player can go ahead and announce a "Mahjong" by revealing the cards.

There are different ways in which a play can be interrupted. The common rule is that there have to be 13 tiles in a player's hand at any given point. This means that if one tile is discarded, it has to be replaced by another tile. If 13 tiles are not present, the player is penalised.

A winning hand simply has 14 tiles. The first winning hand is called "winning by the wall". The second is called "winning by a discard". The rules and regulations keep changing from region to region. They also change according to age.

The Mahjong tiles are piled one on top of the other in certain patterns. A tile with another tile over it cannot be played.

Most people stick to keeping the table to a minimum size. Before they can win the game, they need to score points for a "pong" and a "kong", where the first is a set of three identical tiles and the second is a set of four identical tiles.

Before discarding the tiles, a player who has a "kong" may declare it. This is the "hidden kong". If there are three matching tiles and there is one discarded tile in hand, it is called "kong by discard". The player with the highest score wins the game.

Fact card

- There are more than 20 different variations of Mahjong.
- A player cannot say that they have a Mahjong if they do not. It is not a written rule, but a courtesy rule for fair gameplay.
- Superstitions are common among players. Some believe that they should change their underwear after a loss.

Go

Go is yet another strategic board game from China. It is played between two players. Also popularly known as a game of stones due to the nature of the pieces involved in it, Go is a very popular game around the world today.

Origin

This game originated more than 2500 years ago in China. It is supposed to be one of the four most essential arts. It reached Korea in the fifteenth century. It then spread to Japan by the seventeenth century. It became a popular board game in the west by the nineteenth century. In the earlier times, go was believed to be a fortune-telling device. Ancient Chinese and Japanese art have shown people playing this game. It is also a part of the literature. The size of the board underwent many changes. Today, the 19 ×19 board is the standard size.

Rules

The rules of this game are mainly focussed on the order of play and the scoring system. The two most essential rules in this game are "the rule of liberty" and the "ko rule". The game is played with black and white stones.

Each stone on the table should have at least one point next to it, either above it, below it or to its sides. Therefore, a stone or a group of stones that move from their liberty have to be moved out of the board. Stones on the board cannot repeat their previous position.

Apart from the afore-mentioned rules, almost all the other rules change as per the pattern of the game.

A good thing about this game is that the weaker players, or those just learning the game, are given two extra stones. Players must place the stones on the board in an alternating pattern of white-black-white, in all directions.

The stones are arranged diagonally to form a chain. The chain can be expanded, but in the same way. A vacant point adjacent to a stone is called "liberty". A stone chain has to have minimum liberty, otherwise it is captured.

The stones are placed on the lines rather than in the squares on the board. The squares just measure the distance.

Passing, suicide and komi are the three most important scoring moves in the game.

Fact card

- Go is called "Igo" in Japan.
- Japan has built the largest board for Go which is 40 × 40 m.
- This game is considered to be excellent for children because they get the opportunity to develop their beginner's skills.
- Players in this game are not allowed to make a move which returns any portion of the board to the previous position. This is considered a foul move.